The Cutest Nature Book ever!

Your guide to crafting, daydreaming, writing, and thinking in the great outdoors.

by Carrie Anton
illustrated by Jen Skelley

★ American Girl®

Published by American Girl Publishing, Inc.
Copyright © 2010 by American Girl, LLC

Questions or comments? Call 1-800-845-0005, visit our Web site at **americangirl.com**, or write to Customer Service, American Girl, 8400 Fairway Place, Middleton, WI 53562-0497.

Printed in China

10 11 12 13 14 15 LEO 10 9 8 7 6 5 4 3 2 1

All American Girl marks are trademarks of American Girl, LLC.

Editorial Development: Carrie Anton

Art Direction and Design: Camela Decaire

Production: Judith Lary, Jeannette Bailey, Kendra Schluter, Sarah Boecher, Tami Kepler

Illustrations: Jen Skelley

Photography: Radlund Studios

Stylists: Carrie Anton and Camela Decaire

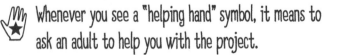

Whenever you see a "helping hand" symbol, it means to ask an adult to help you with the project.

Dear Reader,

It's a great big world out there, and nature offers so many cool objects to collect, fun places to explore, and things to excite the senses. But let's face it: once you get outside, you can find yourself saying, "Now what?" With this book, that question is answered.

The Cutest Nature Book Ever! is your personal guide to becoming an explorer of the great outdoors—but not in a school science-project sort of way. Through art projects, crafts, fun writing tasks, and Collection Challenges, you're about to embark on a new adventure!

Let's get started.

Your friends at American Girl

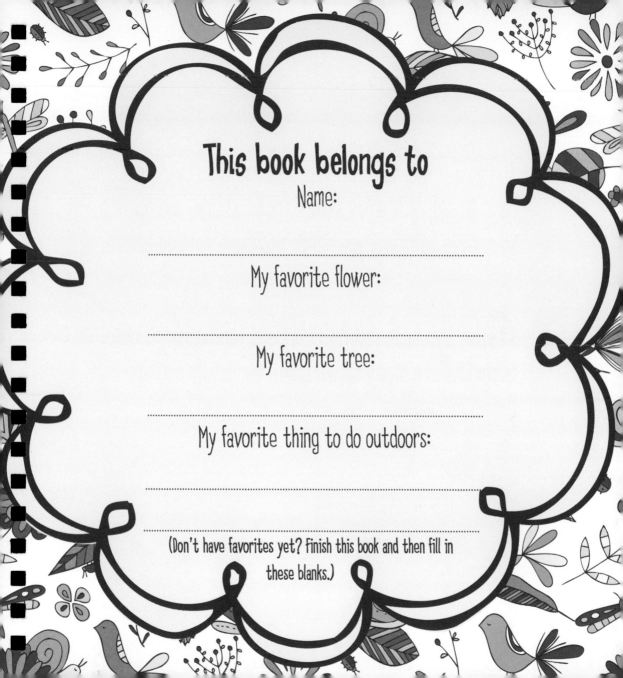

This book belongs to

Name:

....

My favorite flower:

....

My favorite tree:

....

My favorite thing to do outdoors:

....

(Don't have favorites yet? Finish this book and then fill in these blanks.)

How to Use This Book

1. The goal is NOT to finish this book fast. Instead, use this book to help you enjoy nature, get outside, and open your eyes to things you never may have noticed before.

2. Reading this book several times and repeating various activities are highly encouraged—especially during different seasons.

3. The pages of this book are just filled with ideas. If you think of something better to do instead of what is suggested, DO IT! There are no rules for your imagination (unless your parents say so—what they say goes).

4. Write, paint, doodle, and store things in this book. Really, it's OK!

5. And the last and most important point:

Have fun!

Favorite Outdoor Places

Make a list of all the outdoor places you most enjoy and why you love each one. Your list can include parks, backyards, vacation spots, secret spots, and anyplace you love to go that is not in a building.

1. ....

I love it because ....

....

2. ....

I love it because ....

....

and Why You Love Them

3. ....

I love it because...

....

4. ....

I love it because...

....

5. ....

I love it because...

....

Creating an Outdoor Space Just for You

You probably already have an indoor space that's all your own, such as a favorite reading chair, a fort made with pillows and blankets, or even just your bed. Now take time to create a place outside that gives you the same calm and cozy feelings as your inside space.

Do you have a yard?

If the answer is yes, you have lots of options.
(If the answer is no, head to the next question.)

- Set up a lawn chair in the shade.

- With a parent's permission, string some pretty outdoor lights on a low-hanging branch, and spread out a blanket below for a nice nighttime spot.

- Search for the most perfect grassy spot and simply take a seat!

Do you have a porch, deck, or balcony?

If the answer is yes, here are some ideas made just for you.
(If the answer is no, skip to the last question.)

• A fold-up beach chair and table are nice for small spaces
and can be put away when not in use.

• Ask Mom or Dad for a great big pillow to plop down upon.
(Be sure to sweep or wipe up any dirt first.)

Have only a window
to the outside world?

Don't fret—there's still hope!

• Pack a blanket, some water, and a book (such as THIS book) in a bag.
Head to a nearby park with your family or friends.

• Create a cozy seat with pillows near a window.
(Yes, this is technically indoors, but opening a window lets the outside in!)

Two-Minute Collection

Grab a stopwatch.

It's time for your first Collection Challenge!

Go to an outdoor space and set two minutes on the clock. In those two minutes, collect all the flat nature stuff you can find. Then jump to the bottom of the page for the second half of the challenge.

OK, ready? Set? COLLECT!

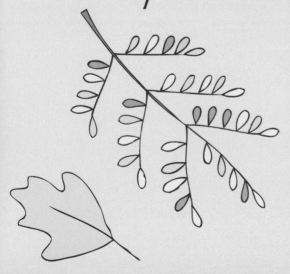

Welcome back!

Flat Stuff Craft Challenge

Using a glue stick or some double-sided tape, make a fun picture using your flat finds. Here are some picture ideas: butterflies, hearts, stars, funny faces, or houses.

Date: .... Place Collected: ....

See a Tree

There are all kinds of trees, such as oaks, elms, dogwoods, maples, and pines. What kinds of trees live near you? Do a little research and list all the trees as you see them.

....

....

....

Make a tree rubbing.

You'll need a tree (of course!), a crayon, the next page, and maybe an extra set of hands (those hands can be attached to a friend, sibling, parent, etc.). Place the next page against the trunk of a tree, and hold it in place while you rub a crayon lightly over the paper. The patterns of the bark should appear.

Date:........................... Place Rubbed: ....

Press a Leaf

Pressed leaves are pretty and so easy!

See for yourself:

1. Look outside for a leaf you like. Make sure that it isn't wet or moldy.

2. Take a sheet of newsprint and tear it in half.

3. Sandwich the leaf between the two pieces of newsprint. Then put the paper in between this page and that page. ⟶

4. Close the book—WAIT! Don't close it until you finish reading this part. When the book is closed, pile on a few heavy books. Come back in two days and check out your super-smooshed creation!

Make your leaves last!

1. Place each of your pressed leaves between two pieces of wax paper.

2. Ask an adult to run a medium-hot iron slowly over the wax paper for about 10 seconds. Note: use a cloth between the wax paper and the iron.

3. Let cool before removing the leaves from the wax paper.

September
leaves

Craft Time: Nature's Greetings

Pressed leaves are lovely to look at all on their own. And on a card to help brighten someone's day, they're even more perfect! Now that you've become an expert leaf presser, put your skills to good use.

Using a glue stick or double-sided tape, attach leaves in pretty patterns to a piece of folded card stock. Embellish your card with stickers, ribbons, buttons, or whatever you can think up! Need some ideas? Look over there. ➝

Leftover Leaves?

Quick! Think of four more crafts you could make
or things you could decorate with leaves.

1. Picture Frame

2.

3.

4.

Twiggy Things

What if you had a pile of twigs instead of leaves?
What four things would you make or decorate instead?

1...

2...

3...

4...

Good job! Go make one of the crafts from
either of your lists.

Pick-Up Sticks

Chores? In a book that's supposed to be about having fun? Nah! This isn't a trick to get you to do yard work. This is the old game Pick-Up Sticks played with real sticks instead of plastic ones.

1. With one or more friends, gather a bunch of small sticks all about the same size.

2. Take all of the found sticks and drop them onto an outdoor flat surface. Don't rearrange any of the sticks once they've landed.

3. Each player, one at a time, will pick up a stick without moving any of the other sticks in the pile. If a stick moves, the player's turn is over and the stick stays in the pile. If no sticks move, the player gets to go again. The player with the most sticks when the pile is gone wins.

Stick Painting

Who says you HAVE to use a paintbrush to paint a picture?
Sticks have all sorts of tips, making them fun painting tools.

With different-colored acrylic craft paints, use a stick as you would a paintbrush
to draw a picture on this page. Let the paint dry before closing the book.

Date: .... Place Painted: ....

Craft Time: Perfectly Perched

Whooo's that sweet tweet sitting upon your branch?

You can make a little feathered friend to top a twig. It's really easy!

Photocopy the shapes on this page to use as patterns, or make your own. Then cut the shapes out from felt. Use craft or fabric glue to attach the shapes to a large pom-pom. Let dry. Use dimensional fabric paint to add eyes.

Dry yet? Good! Now glue your bird to a twig. And let it dry, again. (Wow, there sure is a lot of drying!)

Now sigh and say, "So cute."

You know what would make your birdy super happy? Another buddy to tweet with. (That's a nudge for you to make another one!)

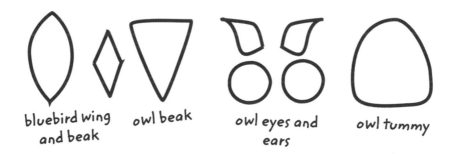

bluebird wing and beak   owl beak   owl eyes and ears   owl tummy

Five-Minute Collection

Collection Challenge Time!

With five minutes on the clock, collect as many different kinds of nature items as you can find—flat, fuzzy, hard, long, whatever!

Ready? Set? COLLECT!

Hello again.
Feathered Friend Craft Challenge

Using the items you brought back (or as many as you can), create a feathered friend. It could be a duck, a crow, an owl, a parrot, or anything else that your collection inspires you to make. Try to see the items you collected in a new way. What would make a good beak? How will you build the body? What could work as wings? Be creative!

cut leaves, nut, twig

IDEAS

milkweed pod and leaves

pussy willow bud, berry, leaf

A Little Birdie Told Me . . .

Imagine you could have a conversation with a bird. Would you ask her how it feels to fly? Or how she builds a nest? Or about all of the places she's visited? How do you think she'd answer?

Use these pages to write a made-up story about a chat between you and your birdie buddy.

Draw a picture of your feathered friend.

Craft-Store Feather Print

Some people say finding a feather is good luck. But no matter how lucky feathers are, you should leave them be! Picking up feathers found in nature is against the law in many states. That doesn't mean all feathers are off-limits. Craft stores offer many kinds of pretty feathers.

Over a piece of scrap paper, carefully paint a very thin layer of craft paint on both sides of the feather. Place the feather on this page and then close the book on top of it. Open up the book again and remove the feather. Let the paint print dry. Turn your print into a work of art by doodling around your feather print to make it into your own creation.

Eight-Minute Collection

Get your trusty stopwatch.

It's time again for a Collection Challenge!

Put eight minutes on the clock. In that amount of time, collect as many pairs of opposites as you can find. That means if you collect something soft, also collect something hard. Or if you find a black object, also search for a white object, and so on.

Ready? Set? COLLECT!

You're back!

Bookmark Craft Challenge

With the items you collected, make a bookmark. Use some of the items on your bookmark or just as themes for your bookmark. On the next page are some examples.

ribbon and acorns!

Story Time

Nature = Inspiration

Go outside and look around you. What do you see? Grass? Leaves? Insects? Sand? Rocks? All on their own, they might not have much meaning. But when you put them together, they tell a story. On these two pages, create a character who lives outside—in the forest, on the beach, in a tree, etc. Describe what your character looks like and where she lives, and don't forget to give her a name. Fill your character's world with details that describe your own outdoor setting: how brightly the sun is shining, what the air smells like after a night of rainfall, or how cool the breeze feels on your face. Get inspired by nature!

more ⤳

_____'s Clothing

Your character's name

Create some wearables for your fictional character.

Draw some outfits below that
she might like to wear.

_____'s Room

Everyone needs a space of her very own.

Draw your character's bedroom below.

Press Small Flowers

Pressed flowers are beautiful on pictures, bookmarks, and note cards, to name just a few things. And they're easy to make!

1. Find small flowers that are OK to pick—no scavenging in your neighbor's prized petunias! Be sure to pick flowers that aren't wet (so don't pick them right after it rains or first thing in the morning when petals may be covered with dew), and look for flowers that don't have wilted petals—those that are brown, wrinkly, or damaged. Thin flowers are easiest to press.

2. Tear a sheet of newsprint in half.

3. Place one piece of the newsprint on the opposite page. Carefully place your flowers facedown on the newsprint, making sure the petals are lying flat. Cover the flowers with the other sheet.

4. Close this book and pile on a few heavy books. Come back in two days and check out your flattened flowers!

Craft Time: Framed Flowers

Filling a frame is one beautiful way to show off your pressed blooms.

Here's what to do:

1. ✋ Open a frame and ask an adult to remove the glass. Use the back piece as a guide. Trace this shape onto a piece of clear self-adhesive vinyl paper (such as Con-Tact® paper), and cut it out.

2. Arrange several flowers on a piece of pretty scrapbook paper that is larger than the shape you cut from the vinyl paper.

3. Remove the backing on the piece of vinyl paper, exposing the sticky side. Gently place the vinyl paper over the flowers and press onto the scrapbook paper, making sure that no bubbles form.

4. Using the vinyl paper as a guide, cut off the excess scrapbook paper.

5. Put the flower picture in the frame. Ask an adult to close up the frame. Display your natural art, or give it as a pretty present to someone special.

Ten-Minute Collection

It's stopwatch time!
Here's your final timed Collection Challenge.

With ten minutes on the clock, collect as many interesting stones and pebbles as you can find. Look for different shapes, sizes, and textures.

Ready? Set? COLLECT!

Ten minutes up already? You rock!

Garden Stone Craft Challenge

In addition to your stones, you'll need a brick, craft paint, a paintbrush, and craft glue. Start by washing and drying the stones you collected and then painting them (over a covered surface, of course). Once the paint is dry, arrange the stones on the brick (which you can also paint) to make a work of art. Use craft glue to hold the stones in place. When dry, set the brick in your garden as a decoration. If you don't have a garden or outdoor space, use the brick as a doorstop or make two to use as bookends.

Your Name Rocks!

And don't you forget it!

Create a fun way to display your name in your room. Spell out your name using pebbles and stones, gluing them to a piece of card stock. Run back outside (unless you're crafting in the great outdoors) and pick up lots of little sticks. Glue your sticks and twigs onto a plain frame. Once it's dry, put the frame around your rock name and "stick" it in your room.

Rock Insects

These bugs are nothing but cute!

Some people think that insects are icky and scary. And maybe they're right. OR maybe they just haven't met the right bugs.

Use glue and craft supplies, such as felt, chenille stems, acrylic paint, and googly eyes, to craft up some cute, funny bugs. Look around outside to see all the different kinds of insects you can make—spiders, ladybugs, ants, beetles, flies, butterflies, and more. Just don't touch . . . let them "bee"!

Creepy Crawlers

Bugs are everywhere—even on these pages!

Using an ink pad, fill these pages with finger- and thumbprints. Let the ink dry. (Wash your hands!) Doodle your finger- and thumbprints into all kinds of bugs.

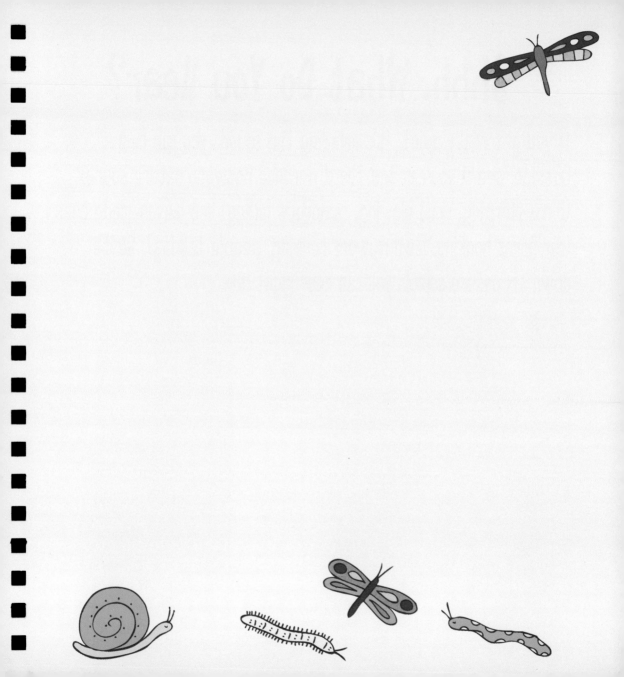

Shhh. What Do You Hear?

If you get really quiet, it's amazing the sounds you can hear. Outside, see if you can tell the difference between nature sounds (birds chirping, wind blowing, raindrops falling) and human-made ones (car horns honking, lawn mowers running, people talking). Write down six nature sounds you can hear right now.

1. ....

2. ....

3. ....

4. ....

5. ....

6. ....

Imagine what your favorite nature sound
would look like if it were an object instead
of a sound. Draw it here.

Finding Faces

Have you ever looked up at the clouds and felt sure there was a face staring back at you? Clouds aren't the only places where you can find faces. Just look at things that create patterns, such as tree bark, flower petals, or rock piles, and you're likely to find a face. Capture the face images with a camera, and tape or glue your pictures here.

Hmmm. That Looks Different

Remember the special outside space you set up earlier in the book? When was the last time you were there? If it has been more than two weeks, it's time to make another visit. That's because things are always changing in nature. Sometimes a particular tree will have more leaves or those leaves will be a different color. Sometimes the water level of a pond will be lower than at other times. The more you visit this special place, the more you'll see—and hear and smell.

Complete the following sections on different days and times to see how your special outdoor space is changing. Track anything that you notice is different, such as the color of the sky, the feel of the grass, or the smells in the air. Notice things that were there before but now are missing, as well as the new things that have arrived.

Date: ....

Weather: ....

Changes: ....

....

....

Date: ....

Weather: ....

Changes: ....

....

....

Date: ....

Weather: ....

Changes: ....

....

....

Date: ....

Weather: ....

Changes: ....

....

....

Date: ....

Weather: ....

Changes: ....

....

....

Date: ....

Weather: ....

Changes: ....

....

....

Date: ....

Weather: ....

Changes: ....

....

....

Date: ....

Weather: ....

Changes: ....

....

....

Date: ....

Weather: ....

Changes: ....

....

....

Date: ....

Weather: ....

Changes: ....

....

....

Date: ....

Weather: ....

Changes: ....

....

....

Date: ....

Weather: ....

Changes: ....

....

....

Date: ....

Weather: ....

Changes: ....

....

....

Date: ....

Weather: ....

Changes: ....

....

....

Date: ....

Weather: ....

Changes: ....

....

When you run out of room here, start your own nature notebook!

Celebrate Nature

Do you know who deserves a party? Mother Nature! List three reasons why you'd throw Mother Nature a party:

1. ....

2. ....

3. ....

OK, it's time to celebrate!

Your final Collection Challenge is to find as many things as possible to use as decorations for your party. Try using:

- leaves and fabric paint to stamp designs on napkins.
- dried flowers and twigs on place cards.
- wildflowers in a rain boot as a centerpiece.
- acorns and ribbons as napkin ties.

How did you get creative with nature? Send letters to:
The Cutest Nature Book Ever! Editor
American Girl
8400 Fairway Place, Middleton, WI 53562

Here are some other American Girl books you might like:

❑ I read it.

❑ I read it.

❑ I read it.

❑ I read it.

❑ I read it.

Visit americangirl.com
and click on **Fun for Girls**
for quizzes and games.

Place
Stamp
Here

American Girl®
PO BOX 620497
MIDDLETON WI 53562-0497